הֲלִיכוֹת בֵּיתָהּ

THE
WAYS OF HER HOUSEHOLD

A PRACTICAL HANDBOOK FOR JEWISH WOMEN
ON TRADITIONAL CUSTOMS AND OBSERVANCES

BY

HARRIS M. LAZARUS, M.A.

Rabbi of the Brondesbury Synagogue, and Assistant Dayan
to the United Synagogue, London.

Part 1: On woman's duties and activities in the Jewish
household.

Part 2: On the personal duties of a Jewish wife.

PART II.

LONDON:
MYERS AND CO.,
59, HIGH HOLBORN, W.C. 1.
1923.

PART II.

*On the Personal Duties of a Jewish Wife appertaining
to the Laws of Niddah (separation)
and Toharah (purity).*

"For commandment is a lamp
and teaching is light ;

"And reproofs of instruction
are the way of life."

Proverbs, vi. 23.

CONTENTS.

CONTENTS

CHAPTER I.

THE LAWS OF NIDDAH
(SEPARATION)
AND TOHARAH (PURITY).

1. The spirit of these laws. 2. Free from superstition.
3. The Jewish view. 4. Woman's three duties.
5. Moral strength.

The spirit of these laws 1. The laws of "Niddah" (some of which are set out here) have been in practice and in the charge of the Jewish people for thousands of years. These laws have their foundations in the Bible, and traditional interpretation has throughout maintained the original spirit, viz., that of *purity*, *modesty* and *holiness*.

The subject is naturally one of delicacy, and should be approached in a spirit of reverence, especially as we have to consider it from a religious point of view. Jewish teachers, at all times, have discussed these matters—on their Biblical

2—B

basis—with sympathy and practical knowledge, and have not lost sight of the dignity of Jewish womanhood. "The daughters of Israel—said they—are holy and pure."

Free from superstition 2. We are proud to assert, in these days of scientific progress and enlightenment, that our traditional teachings have ever been kept free from the superstitious absurdities which have been rife in the minds of other peoples on these matters, and we must reject every attempt of the ignorant and prejudiced to associate our holy practices with their fancies or with any unworthy motive of separating and degrading woman on account of her physical infirmity.*

The Jewish view 3. According to the Jewish teachings, fully in accord with

*Maimonides, the eminent Jewish sage, philosopher and physician, rejects the superstitious beliefs and customs of the Sabeans, the Magi (Persians) and other Eastern peoples regarding a menstruous woman, and brings out very clearly, by contrast, the spirltual side and the grades of holiness and purity in these observances, as conceived in Judaism.—"Guide for the Perplexed," Book iii. chapter 47. (Dr. Friedlander's Translation, p. 368).

those of science, her monthly "courses"
are part of her physical nature : they are
a physiological and not a pathological
phenomenon. Man and woman—according to the Jewish conception of life—
God made them both ; equal partners in
life's destiny, each adapted for the fulfil-
ment of his or her part, according to the
Divine and all-wise plan ; both subject to
laws and restraints which are intended to
make their lives nobler and holier.

Woman's "three duties" 1. The observance of the laws
of " niddah " is associated in our
traditional teachings with two others, viz.,
the setting apart of the dough-gift—*Chal-
lah*, and the kindling of the Sabbath-
lights in the home, and these duties are
not, as already explained, a derogatory
reflection on woman's weakness, but
rather an indication of her strength and
the latent potentialities for good which
are present in woman's nobler self. Nay,
as Jews proud of our heritage, as the
people who produced and gave the Bible
to the world, we must reject the thought-
less, uncurbed licentiousness which alas,
according to the testimony of many

medical writers on these subjects so often
prevails in the relationship between man
and woman in the world around us.
Perhaps, it is due to the absence of such
authoritative guidance which Jewish Tradition affords.

Moral strength   5. These laws have been to us
a safeguard to health, and a
source of moral strength.* The minute
attention that is expected to be given to
these observances has led to the creation
of that sympathetic understanding

*It is interesting to read the following remarks of a
physician of many years' standing and experience : "The
laws prescribed by Moses are observed still, by the
greater number of Jewesses. In the great capitals,
indeed, there is still some probable laxity, and it is noted
that there, too, the primitive types are gradually becom-
ing effaced, which is perhaps owing in part to this very
circumstance ... If we compare the Hebraic legislation
with that of the Egyptians and Hindoos, we shall be
struck by the fact that Moses greatly simplified the practices of purification, suppressing all founded on superstition and maintaining only that which was really useful to
hygiene and favourable to morals. But the purity of
blood conduced to another end of an infinitely superior
order : it was the symbol of interior purity . . ."—Augustus
K. Gardner, M.D. (Professor of Clinical Midwifery in
New York Medical College) "The Conjugal Relation-
ships," seventh edition, pp. 137-138, London, Simpkins
Marshall & Co., Ltd., 1914.

between husband and wife which is characteristic of the Jewish home, and to the cultivation of considerateness and a modest reserve—the basis of that personal dignity and mutual respect which husband and wife owe to each other.

Chapter II.

REGULAR MENSES (Courses).

1. Niddah—its meaning. 2. Prohibition and exhortation.
   3. Separation. 4. Anticipatory separation. 5. Niddah-separation. 6. The "five days." 7. The
   "seven pure days." 8. Synagogue attendance and
   prayers.

"Niddah" its meaning 1. The Hebrew word "niddah" means literally, a state-of-separation or withdrawal : hence it is used to denote a woman during the time of her menses, as one who is in a state of-separation or withdrawal.

Prohibition and exhortion 2. The Bible forbids conjugal association during the whole time of " niddah-separation " as an iniquitous, abominable contamination ; a heinous and immoral offence almost on a par with idolatry. (Cp. Lev. xviii. 19-30 and xx. 18, and Ezek. xviii. 5, 6 ff.)

Holy Writ demands that Israel shall avoid all unholy practices which are an

" abomination unto the Lord " and it exhorts the Jewish people to make every endeavour to uphold their personal and national sanctity. (Cp. Lev. xxviii. 7-8, 22-26).

Separation 3. Traditional teaching emphatically demands a temporary separation between husband and wife at the time of her " menses." A certain distance has to be maintained. Modesty, self-respect and the laws of hygiene, no less than the Bible and Tradition, demand it.* Their mutual affection and regard will not suffer thereby. Nay, they stand to gain much more by the observance of this demand made by modesty and religion, than by the relaxation of their requirements. (See paragraph 8.)

Anticipatory separation 4. Traditional practice has established a period of 12 hours

---

*It is interesting to note how a free, fearless and independent scientist like Dr. Marie Carmichael Stopes gives ready recognition and support to the Biblical Law and our ancient traditional practice as a result of her latest research in these matters. " The results obtained by my independent investigation—she says—thus find some support in this ancient wisdom of the East." See " Married Love " pp. 70-72, eleventh edition, Putnam and Sons, Ltd., 1923.

(day or night) as an *anticipatory* period of
separation. Conjugal association is just
then to be avoided. But, when the usual
time has already arrived and passed, and
the rest of that day (or night) too has gone
by without any visible sign of the actual
onset of the expected "menses" appear-
ing, the prohibition lapses, and the privil-
eges of marital companionship need not,
any longer, on that account, be restricted.

Niddah-Separation 5. As soon as the slightest
definite indication has been
noticed of the coming "menses" the state
of "niddah-separation" commences.
This state of separation extends over a
period of not less than 12 days consisting
of, at least five days of the "menses" and
seven subsequent days, usually designated
as "the seven days of purification" or
"pure days."

The "five days" 6. Towards the end of the fifth
day, before sunset, it has to be
carefully ascertained that the discharge
has by that time completely ceased. This
fact has to be established beyond doubt.
and not until then, can the "seven pure

days " be commenced, by the following
morning.   Here the following two points
should be noted carefully :

(a) The examination on the fifth (or
subsequent) day must take place
towards the end of the day, but
before sunset, that is to say, *by
daylight* and not at dusk or dark,
by artificial light.

(b) The evening counts always as the
beginning of the following day,*
Thus, if the "menses" began,
say, on Saturday evening, or at
any time during the next day, it
is all counted as Sunday, and
the fifth day for the necessary
investigating examination is
Thursday before sunset.

"The seven days of purifica-
tion"   7. The seven days of purification are most important.   When
the result of the examination is
altogether satisfactory, her person is ren-

*Thus, Friday evening is the beginning of Sabbath
and Saturday evening the beginning of week-days.
Cp. Genesis, i. 5, 8, etc., and Lev. xxiii. 32 (with reference
to the Day of Atonement "In the ninth day of the
month, at even, from even unto even shall ye keep your
Sabbath ").

dered freshly clean,* in readiness for the
seven pure days which are to begin by
the next morning. Daily, morning and
evening, the inspection is repeated.
Many piously carry out the Bible's instruction literally "Then she shall number to herself seven days." (Leviticus. xv.
28). Accordingly they count expressly
each day :—"This is the first, second,
third, etc., of the seven pure days," a
practice which certainly helps one to
characterise the observance as a spiritual
exercise. At the termination of the
seventh day the *Mikveh* is visited, (See
chapter iv. 3-6).

Restrictions 8. Throughout these 12 days
of "niddah-separation" the separation
between husband and wife should be continued conscientiously. The customary
little caresses are suspended for the time
being and such contact as might lead to
these is avoided sedulously.

*Even though this should happen to be on the eve of
the Fast of the Ninth of Ab, or during the week of
Shivah mourning when bathing in warm water is con-
sidered a forbidden pleasure, this circumstance is con-
sidered as necessary and essential, and is permitted
accordingly.

Synagogue attendance and prayers 9. Biblical law forbids a woman during the time of "niddah-separation" and after childbirth to enter the Sanctuary, to handle or touch holy things connected with the worship, holy meat or the dues that were given to the priests. (Levitic. Chap. xii. 19-31.)* Some felt that these restrictions of the national Sanctuary should be continued and applied to the Synagogue and its worship. But, extreme views have not met with general approval. At no time should she feel herself debarred from uttering prayer and praise to her Heavenly Father. Holy thoughts are uplifting and purifying, acceptable to God at all times, whenever they fill our minds and move our hearts. (On visiting the synagogue after childbirth see Chapter iii. 6).

---

*Maimonides, the Jewish sage, in the passage already referred to above (in the introduction), endeavours to show that these and other kindred laws in connection with the Temple were necessary and especially intended to maintain due reverence and sanctity of the House of God. No person was allowed to enter it unprepared, without previous special purification and even the priests who were on active service in the Temple, in the course of their services had to purify themselves repeatedly. (See Ex. xxx. 17-21).

CHAPTER III.

IRREGULAR AND CASUAL
OCCURRENCES.

"The daughters of Israel are holy and pure."
Midrash Sifre.

1. Regular and irregular. 2. The law in practice—
indications—colours—favourable colours—doubtful
cases. 3. Casual stains. 4. During the first three
of the "pure days." 5. After childbirth.
6. Thanksgiving after childbirth.

Regular and Irregular 1. The indications, duration of the menses and interval between one monthly period and the next, vary in different persons. There is generally (in healthy persons) a certain amount of regularity, and therefore, the time for anticipatory separation (as described in the preceding chapter §4) can, more or less easily be determined. It is the irregular interval and casual occurrences which give rise to complicated questions in respect to the law of "separation." It is, indeed, beyond the scope of this hand-

book to deal with these delicate problems
at any length ; but, at least, the main
directions and principles should be clearly
indicated and understood.

The law in practice   2. Holy Writ sets out the laws
of regular and irregular con-
ditions (Lev. xv. 19-28).   The questions
involved in these few verses are rather
complicated, and our sages have discussed
them with reverence, care and consideration.   It is with pride, however, that
they declare that " the daughters of Israel
have of themselves adopted a practical,
strict and uniform standard."   The principles in practice will be set out here
respectfully, as simply and shortly as the
subject will allow :—

Indications   (a) The slightest sensation or
indication which suggests the pos-
sibility of a commencing discharge demands an immediate
investigation.   If this is not
done, the state of " niddah "
must be assumed.

Colours   (b) The slightest show of
colour, be it of the faintest, a

mere speck of red, dark-red or
even blackish, constitutes a state
of " niddah."—Cp. chapt. i. 5.

Favourable colours

(c) On the other hand, a col-
ourless discharge (whites), or one
of a light-brown (coffee or chest-
nut), yellow, greenish or bluish
tint, does *not* constitute a state
of " niddah."

Doubtful cases

(d) There are other shades
which are either difficult to
determine or on which the
opinion of authorities differ, such
as, for instance, dark-brown and
orange. If, with all due modesty
and reserve as befits this delicate
matter, guidance can be obtained
from a competent authority, it
should be sought. But if this is
not possible, the stricter view
should be taken, In all cases of
doubt, or where circumstances
have not permitted a careful examination, the stricter view is
certainly the safest.

Casual stains   3. Traditional practice goes even to greater length, so that if without expectation, sensation or previous indication of any kind, a red stain is discovered on her person, white garment or her immediate personal surroundings, it is taken as constituting a state of " niddah," provided that the following two conditions are present :—

(1) The stain cannot be traced to another cause, and

(2) The stain of a group of small spots near each other, when taken together are of a considerable size. *

But if, on the other hand, this casual and totally unexpected stain (or several smaller ones taken together), be

(a) *Not* of any considerable size*

(b) *Not* actually on white, but on a coloured ground,

(c) *Not* at all in a position as likely to be of menstrual origin, or

*About the size of half a large (butter) bean.

(*d*) Can definitely be traced to some other cause, it is not taken as constituting a state of " niddah."

During the first three "pure days" 4. Should such an unexpected casual stain be discovered during the first three of " the seven pure days " these first three days are lost, and the series has to be recommenced afresh from the next morning, unless the origin is known with absolute certainty.

After childbirth 5. The procedure after child-birth (or miscarriage) is the same as that of ordinary "niddah." Careful investigation must first establish that there is no discharge whatever, before " the seven pure days " may be commenced with the usual care and prep-aration, as described above (Chapter ii. 7).

In any case, the ritual "mikveh" may not be used before the end of the second week (fourteen days) after the confine-ment. Such early convalescence and readiness, however, occur but rarely. The Bible, in fact, prescribes a much longer term of separation—forty days after a male child and twice that number of days

after a female child especially, with
reference to her visiting the Sanctuary in
order to bring her offerings (Levit. xii.
1-8). In some few communities this
longer term of separation is still observed.

**Thanks-
giving
childbirth**   6. It is customary after childbirth to visit the synagogue as
soon as convalescence and circumstances
permit, in order to render thanks for the
recovery and to offer prayer on behalf of
the newly-born child.   Often, if conve-
nient, the child accompanies the mother.
Should this visit take place on a Sabbath,
the husband is called to the Torah, so that
he too may pronounce publicly the benediction of thanks (Gomel) for her recovery.
(The prayer will be found in the authorised Prayer-book p. 312.)

THE MIKVEH.

The Mikveh 1. The Hebrew word " mikveh " means a (natural) gathering of water. (Cp. Gen. i. 10). In Leviticus, ii. 36, the Bible has a more characteristic passage in which there are mentioned the several kinds of natural gatherings of water that may be used for ritualistic purposes :—" Nevertheless a fountain or pit (well) wherein there is a gathering of water shall be clean " (pure). From this text there has been derived the essential traditional principles of the construction of a " mikveh." The details of its construction do not belong here, they concern the Ecclesiastical Authorities who direct its construction. It is, however, necessary to know that an ordinary bath does

not satisfy the traditional, religious requirements of a "mikveh." Besides
other requirements it has to be like a
well sunk in the ground ; it must be wide
and deep enough to enable a person to
dip under easily and to be wholly submerged ; it must contain not less than 40
"seah" of naturally-gathered water before
any other (hot) water may be added by
artificial means. This required amount
of naturally-gathered water for a *kosher*
(proper) "mikveh" has been calculated to
be in English measure, 160 (one hundred
and sixty) imperial gallons.

Its usage 2. As an institution the "mikveh" has significant, spiritual associations
with the hallowed past. Its ritualistic
usage goes back to the ancient days when
Israel was first taught the great principles
of moral purity and religious sanctity. As
the laws of purification were closely connected with the Sanctuary and holy
things, Tradition has preserved the
essential details with scrupulous fidelity.

Like in the ritual washing of the
hands before meals (and prayer) it is not

cleanliness alone that is intended. In the
act of washing the hands there is implied
spiritual preparation, as well as the sanc-
tification of the meal as a hallowed par-
ticipation of the bounties which God in
His goodness abundantly provides. So
also, is the use of the " mikveh " tra-
ditionally associated with the ideals of
cleanliness, purity, modesty and holiness.

**Cleanliness
aids purity** 3. Purity implies cleanliness,
Traditional interpretation of
Scriptural texts lays great stress on this.
Thus, in traditional practice a warm bath
must precede the use of the " mikveh."
The whole body receives the minutest
attention, the eyes, ears, mouth, teeth,
etc. The hair must be washed and
thoroughly loosened ; the nails must be
trimmed neatly ; foreign bodies, such as
artificial teeth, rings, ear-rings, bandage
or plaster must be set aside. Stains of
ink, dye or tar, etc., or any adhesion of
dough, clay or resin, etc , must be re-
moved before the " mikveh " can be used
effectually, as the final act in the process
of religious purification. Therefore, on
the day when the " mikveh " is to be

visited, women avoid handling any clammy substance which might, unawares, adhere to the fingers. They even avoid eating (animal) food, fish or meat, because the fibres often remain between the teeth, unless that day be Sabbath or Yomtov, when meat is part of the day's order.

Time of bathing 4. The preparatory bathing just decribed above, should take place on the last of "the seven pure days" towards the end of the day. It should begin preferably whilst it is still light and should be performed leisurely, with deliberation. Save only under difficult circumstances may this be put off till dark.

In this connection the following should be noted) :—

The eve of Sabbaths and Festivals (*a*) If the seventh day fall on *Erev-Shabbos* (Friday) or *Erev-Yomtov* the preparatory bathing may *not* be delayed till nightfall, as this certainly involves a breach of the sanctity of the Sabbath or Festival : a warm bath is not permissible on Sabbaths or Festivals, for well-founded reasons.

Sabbath or Festival (*b*) If the seventh day fall on Sabbath or the second day of a Festival, the preparatory bath should be taken on Friday or on the day before Yomtov (*Erev-Yomtov*), due attention being given to all requirements and the "mikveh" should not be used till some time after the termination of the Sabbath or Festival. Even then, some preliminary attention should again be given to the preparation, before actually descending to the "mikveh"

Sabbath-lights (*c*) On *Erev-Shabbos* (Friday) care has to be taken about lighting of the Sabbath lights. No difficulty arises about the Yomtov lights, as these may be lit on her return home; but on Friday evening this is impossible. Therefore, if the preparatory bathing is performed at home, and the "mikveh" is not far from the house, the Sabbath lights might be kindled con ditionally, before setting out for the "mikveh." Otherwise, it is far better to arrange that the husband should light them at the proper time in her absence. (See Part I. chapter vi., on the Sabbath-lights, §§11 and 12.

Submersion
(Tevilah)
5. It is obvious that after such careful preparations a mere perfunctory dipping in the "mikveh" would be entirely contrary to the spirit of the ceremony. Purity, cleanliness, modesty and holiness are its four cardinal points. Neither haste nor nervous discomfort should mar the religous act. Modesty and holy intentions as well as reverence for our ancient, sacred traditions have brought us hither : it is for purity's sake and religious sanctity that the descent is made to the deep well—the "Mikveh."

Thus having descended and taken up a firm, natural, erect position in the water, the whole body is submerged, deliberately and completely, without nervously clutching at anything, or tightly compressing eyes or lids. Then, folding her arms and with uplifted heart, as it were, the follow-

ing benediction is pronounced in Hebrew,
(the attendant prompting if necessary) :—

Blessed art Thou, O
Lord, our God, King of
the Universe, Who hast
hallowed us by Thy
commandments, and
hast bidden us to ob-
serve the ceremony of
Tevilah-Submersion.

בָּרוּךְ אַתָּה יְיָ אֱלֹהֵינוּ
מֶלֶךְ הָעוֹלָם אֲשֶׁר
קִדְּשָׁנוּ בְּמִצְוֹתָיו וְצִוָּנוּ
עַל הַטְּבִילָה :

NOTE : Many dip under a second time after the
benediction has been pronounced. As a rule, a
Jewish woman (generally the attendant) stands
at the side to assist, if necessary, as well as to
see that the submersion is complete, especially
the head and hair.

The proper time   6. The right time for using the
"mikveh" is at the termination
of the seventh day after nightfall, that is,
after the stars have become visible in
the sky.   Only under exceptional circumstances might this be done at an earlier
hour, on the eighth day.   It is not cor-
rect to defer the visit to the "mikveh"
unnecessarily beyond the seventh day, nor
to anticipate ordinarily, even on the eighth
day the hour of Tevilah-submersion, i.e.,
before actual nightfall.

Reserve and modesty   7. It is well to mention here (though perhaps obvious) that all observances connected with " niddah " should be kept within the strictest reserve, that is to say, within the knowledge of those only who are entitled to be informed, of those who are directly concerned, husband and wife. Modesty and reverence demand it. And, as far as they two are concerned, will not this knowledge held in confidence between them, enhance and strengthen their companionship? Will it not deepen their sympathies and devotion which man and wife owe to each other? Is it not, thus, in the power of woman to hallow the bonds of marriage and raise wifehood above a mere compact for convenience and pleasure? Our sages said :- If man and woman live worthily and purely, the Divine Presence abides in their midst.

CHAPTER V.

THE BRIDE.

Introductory.

A mother's duty to her child Jewish mothers cannot allow their daughters to remain ignorant of their duties and responsibilities of wife-hood, since traditional Judaism assigns to the mother, or to some true friend who takes her place, the responsible task of having to apprise the bride of the sacred duties which devolve upon her as a wife, in addition to the noble cares which await her in her new sphere as a Home-maker. Love and courtship are beautiful indeed for their tenderness, aided as they are by youthful, hopeful dreams and worthy aspirations. But, yet, life has its realities which have to be met boldly with knowledge, with good cour-

age and with earnest endeavour. Among
the many preparations made before enter-
ing the new realm of the married estate, a
knowledge of our sacred traditional observances should find a foremost place. By
this a young woman will be prepared to
enter into the holy and difficult partner-
ship of marriage equipped with higher
and worthier thoughts about her person,
her place and her duties in the Home
which she is called upon to make and
preserve. She will be made fully conscious
of her womanly dignity and modesty
which her husband, even in their most
intimate companionship, must acknow-
ledge and respect.

Everything appertaining to the laws
of "niddah" as stated in the previous
chapters applies equally, with but one or
two exceptions, to a bride at her marriage.
It is, therefore, necessary to set down
the several points which are especially
applicable to a bride before marriage.

"The seven pure days" 1. When the date of the marriage has been definitely fixed,
a bride has to observe the " seven days of

purification" carefully and strictly, as
described in Chapter II, §7.   This may be
arranged so, that the seventh day should
come but a day or two before the wedding, but not more than four days before.
And perchance, if the wedding had to be
postponed for a short period, the "seven
days of purification" have to be observed anew, close to the wedding day.

The mikveh 2. The "mikveh" is to be
visited and used in the prescribed man-
ner (see Chapter iv. §§4-5) on the seventh
day, but with this difference, that a bride
may attend to this sacred function at any
time on the seventh (or eighth) day at her
convenience, even in the daytime.   Without observing the "seven days of purification" and without proceeding to the
"mikveh," she is at her marriage in a
state of "niddah" absolutely. (Cp. Chapter II, §§5-8).

The marriage 3. The consummation of marriage constitutes a state of
"niddah-separation" for a period of
eleven (instead of twelve) days, i.e., only
four preliminary, and the "seven pure
days."

**Fasting on
the wed-
ding day
morning** 4. It is customary that the
bride and bridegroom fast on
the wedding day until after the
ceremony. If the fast cause too much
distress, a little tea or milk may be taken
to relieve it, but not alcoholic drink.

Its aim 5. The religious custom of
fasting has a practical as well as a spiritual
aim. Convivial toasting on such occa-
sions, frequently leads to undue hilarity,
and in some cases even to slight intoxica-
tion. The fast protects the bride and
bridegroom, at least, and leads them to
higher thoughts, lending solemnity to the
gaieties of the day. The bridal pair stand
at the threshold of a new life. It is
rightly made an occasion for reviewing
the past and reflecting on the future.
"We do not succeed to higher things,"
said a Jewish sage, "without our sins
being first forgiven." Thus, on the wed-
ding-day, sometime before the ceremony,
the bride and bridegroom read selected
passages from the penitential service of
the Day of Atonement (Authorised
Prayer-book, pp. 258-263).

The result of endeavour   6. In this connection it is not out of place to quote another Talmudic passage. Quoting Leviticus ii. 44 :—"Sanctify yourselves therefore and be ye holy" our sages, explained it thus—"Whosoever sanctifies himself even but little is led to sanctify himself much; whosoever sanctifies himself on earth is aided thereto by Heaven; whosoever sanctifies himself in this (present) world will come sanctified in the world to come."

Concluding words   7. In conclusion, delicate as are all the matters which are dealt with in this section, essentials could not have been omitted. The requirements of our holy Traditions have been set out in a spirit of reverence and with every *consideration for the dignity of Jewish womanhood.*

" Express " Printers, 89, Commercial Street, London, E. 1.